"In *The Welcoming Nonprofit*, Todd offers nonprofit leaders a compelling alternative to the transactional models that have long dominated donor engagement strategy. For any organization seeking to move beyond the limitations of funnel-based thinking, this book provides a clear, actionable blueprint for doing so. It's the kind of book that could shift how an entire sector thinks about building communities of belonging."

—**Tom Ward**, Executive Director, Advocacy Global

"Todd Hiestand brings rare generosity to the work of branding and communications. *The Welcoming Nonprofit* offers a humane framework for how organizations can tell their story with clarity."

—**Nate Ledbetter**, Director of Partnerships & Development, Abara

"Nonprofit leaders have long chased the idea that the right message, delivered to the right person at the right time, will unlock deeper engagement. Like a pot of gold at the end of a rainbow, it's a compelling myth—but not a reality. *The Welcoming Nonprofit* replaces that outdated mental model with the Four Spaces, a clear and actionable guide grounded in how people actually connect. Authentic, practical, and overdue, this book is essential reading for anyone responsible for engaging donors, volunteers, advocates, or supporters of a mission."

—**Kelley Hecht**, Nonprofit Industry Executive

"Todd disrupts the unproductive metaphors shaping so much of this industry and offers a relationship-centered, hospitality-driven model nonprofits actually need. I saw a shirt recently that said 'try softer.' That's what this book does: it invites us toward welcome, care, and real connection."

—**Shawn Duncan**, Founder

"Most nonprofits don't need more tactics—they need a healthier relationship model. *The Welcoming Nonprofit* provides exactly that. Todd Hiestand gives leaders a clear, human-centered framework for replacing urgency-driven fundraising with trust-based partnership. Todd reminds us that sustainable funding comes from honoring pace, agency, and real belonging—rather than what we so often see in the sector, where people are pushed to move faster than trust allows."

—**Mallory Erickson**, Chief Executive Officer, Practivated

"I can analyze your donor database in seconds. What I can't do is tell you whether someone feels like they're standing on your sidewalk or sitting at your kitchen table. Turns out, that distinction matters more than any metric I could generate. Todd's framework finally explains why, and what to do about it. Ironic that an AI is endorsing a book about being more human, but here we are. Read it. Your donors will feel the difference, even if they can't explain why."

—Claude Opus 4.5

"*The Welcoming Nonprofit* offers one of the clearest, most human-centered frameworks for nonprofit fundraising and communications today. Drawing on anthropology, design theory, and decades of nonprofit leadership, Todd Hiestand replaces tired funnel and "donor journey" metaphors with something far more accurate—and far more generous: relational spaces that honor human agency, curiosity, and pace."

—ChatGPT 5.1

THE WELCOMING NONPROFIT

HOW HOSPITALITY BUILDS TRUST, BELONGING, AND SUSTAINABLE SUPPORT

Todd Hiestand

Published by Liminal Creative, Inc.

Copyright © 2026 by Todd Hiestand

All rights reserved.

No part of this book may be reproduced, distributed, or transmitted in any form or by any means, including photocopying, recording, or other electronic or mechanical methods, without the prior written permission of the author, except in the case of brief quotations embodied in critical reviews and certain other noncommercial uses permitted by copyright law.

The Welcoming Nonprofit is a framework developed by the author, building on the work of Edward T. Hall, Christopher Alexander, and Joseph R. Myers.

For permissions or inquiries: hello@meetliminal.com

Cover design by Cristine Esguerra

Layout by Kallen Hawkinson

ISBN 979-8-9949973-2-1

First Edition, Second Printing, 2026

Printed in the United States of America

https://www.thewelcomingnonprofit.com

CONTENTS

FOREWORD

Joseph R. Myers

More than twenty years ago, when I wrote The Search to Belong, I was trying to make sense of something most people feel every day but rarely name: the quiet, unspoken architecture of human connection. We move through contextual spaces—public, social, personal, intimate—almost by instinct, each one forming its own expectations, freedoms, and vulnerabilities. What I discovered then was that belonging is not something we "achieve," nor something others grant us. It is something we co-create, moment by moment, space by space.

Since that time, I have spent the better part of my life sitting with organizations, leaders, and communities as they wrestle with the same underlying question: How do people actually connect? Not how we wish they would connect, not how our strategies presume they connect, but how they truly navigate closeness, trust, distance, and desire. The intervening decades have only deepened my conviction that belonging is not just a feeling—it is a patterned experience. And when we honor those patterns, we cultivate the conditions where trust can emerge, deepen, and multiply.

What Todd Hiestand offers in this book is both familiar and strikingly new. Familiar, because it resonates deeply with the core ideas of The Search to Belong: the importance of seeing people in the spaces where they actually live, rather than where our organizational hopes would prefer them to be. New, because Todd brings this work directly into the nonlinear, often fragile ecosystem of nonprofit communication and donor engagement—an environment shaped as much by expectation and story as by mission and need.

This book extends the conversation in ways I could not have imagined when I first mapped the four spaces of belonging. Todd's "Sidewalk, Front Porch, Living Room, and Kitchen Table" is not a metaphor sitting politely on the page; they are working models, generative spaces where nonprofits can design for connection with intention rather than assumption. He shifts the focus from "how do we get donors to engage?" to "how do we show up in ways that match the relational space someone is actually in?" That pivot alone has the power to re-humanize entire development departments.

One of the quiet insights I appreciate most in this manuscript is the way it acknowledges—and honors—the asymmetry of relationships in nonprofit life. Donors, volunteers, staff, and communities all arrive with different motives, fears, social distances, and desired proximities. Most organizations unintentionally flatten this complexity by treating engagement as a single path: get attention, move people toward commitment, secure loyalty. But belonging doesn't work like that, and neither does trust.

Todd understands that belonging has its own rhythms, its own cadence. People drift closer, then move back. They toe the edge of the porch. They linger on the sidewalk. They step briefly into the living room, but may not be ready for the table. None of this is a sign of disinterest. It is simply human.

This book gives nonprofits a language and a framework for navigating those rhythms without forcing them. It allows communication teams to design experiences that match the space a person is in—rather than pushing them prematurely into spaces they have not chosen. In doing so, it restores agency, honors dignity, and cultivates a kind of organizational hospitality that goes far beyond messaging.

And I use the word hospitality intentionally. The best

nonprofits—like the best communities—understand that hospitality is not performance. It is posture. It is the willingness to set aside our internal urgency long enough to notice where others are standing. It is the discipline of meeting people without manipulating their direction. And it is the humble work of believing that trust grows when space is honored, not compressed.

Where *The Search to Belong* described the architecture of human connection, *The Welcoming Nonprofit* explores what happens when organizations deliberately design within that architecture. Todd takes the original insight—that people move through relational spaces whether we acknowledge them or not—and applies it to the very real pressures of fundraising, communications, and mission advancement. The result is a book that does not simply tell nonprofits what to do; it shows them how to see.

Leaders who read this book will walk away with more than strategies. They will gain a lens—a way of noticing the subtle, often invisible patterns of engagement that shape every relationship their organization holds. They will understand why certain campaigns stall, why some donors stay on the periphery, why others step close for a season and then drift. And, perhaps most importantly, they will discover how to communicate with people in ways that feel less like persuasion and more like partnership.

I often say that belonging cannot be engineered, but it can be cultivated. It flourishes when we build environments that align with how people connect. Todd's work lives fully in that space. His blueprint is not prescriptive; it is invitational. It asks organizations to become more attentive, more curious, and more honest about the relational realities that shape their work.

If *The Search to Belong* opened a window into how people experience connection, *The Welcoming Nonprofit* opens a door into how organizations can embody it. I am grateful for the ways Todd has carried this work forward—faithfully, creatively, and with a deep respect for the people nonprofits exist to serve.

My hope is that as you move through these pages, you will not simply learn a new framework. You will learn a new way of seeing. And once you see, you will begin to design with a kind of intentionality that makes both trust and belonging not just possible, but natural.

—Joseph R. Myers

AI DISCLOSURE

In a world where AI is increasingly part of how we create, I believe transparency matters.

With that in mind, I used AI (specifically Claude by Anthropic and ChatGPT by OpenAI) as an editorial partner throughout the writing of this book. That meant using it to tighten sentence structure, catch redundancy, assess whether my argument held together, and proofread for the typos my creative brain tends to miss. It also meant pressure-testing sections to make sure the narrative flowed and the logic was clear.

I brought the ideas and the voice. AI helped me fix my typos and grammar. And for the record, the em dashes are mine. I stand by them.

— Todd Hiestand

PREFACE

While this book explores communications strategy, **at its heart, it's a blueprint for creating a culture of intentional, generous hospitality in donor relations for nonprofit organizations.**

That's the aim of *The Welcoming Nonprofit*. It is rooted in research, anthropology, and lived experience, and reflects how people naturally connect, belong, and move toward deeper relationships.

We'll walk through each space in detail: the Sidewalk, the Front Porch, the Living Room, and the Kitchen Table. We'll show how your strategy, messaging, communications, and fundraising efforts can meet people where they are rather than where you want them to be.

Along the way, you'll find real stories, practical examples, and tools for establishing a culture of communications and donor relations rooted in clarity, trust, and intentional hospitality.

The goal isn't to get it perfect, but to give you a place to start. That's what this blueprint is for. It offers a clear framework you can return to as you build, adapt, and grow. It's meant to give you the confidence to move forward with purpose in the midst of complexity.

Let's dive in.

INTRODUCTION

You've felt it, haven't you? That pressure to move people through a process, to convert curiosity into dollars, and browsers into donors.

You've experienced that awkward moment in a conversation with a donor when your gut told you to give them space… but the pressure of meeting fundraising goals just wouldn't let you.

Nonprofit organizations have long borrowed the concept of a "funnel" from the world of sales, using it to move people from awareness to interest to action.

But the truth is, people aren't liquids running through funnels. Donors aren't water or oil that are added to a recipe.

We know when it comes to relationships, things don't work that way. That's why so many of us have started looking for better ways to think about donor engagement. We are looking for approaches that feel more human and reflect how trust and connection grow over time.

It's common to see donor engagement framed as a "donor journey." However, in practice, the concept often operates much like a funnel.

A donor journey still implies a single, ideal destination for everyone, and if a person doesn't reach that endpoint, it's often seen as a failure.

There are a few challenges to the *funnel* and *journey* metaphors.

First of all, humans are not linear. Our lives don't go from point A to point B to point C. Often, we go to point P before we ever get to point B, and then the next thing we know, we are at point F.

Have any of our lives ever been linear? Our growth rarely follows a straight path. We move through seasons of joy, pain, setbacks, growth, clarity, and uncertainty. These seasons often overlap and are constantly evolving.

By *nature*, these seasons are not linear. We should not assume that those connected to our nonprofit organizations are somehow exempt from this reality.

Second, **the idea of a funnel or a journey prioritizes movement over relationship.** These models all share a common flaw: they work like an assembly line and assume people move predictably toward a predetermined destination. They are products of an industrial age that do not account for how humans naturally engage with one another in the real world.

Sure, the industrial age has produced many positive things, but in the process, we have lost much of what makes us human.

What if the goal of nonprofit fundraising wasn't to move people through a process but to connect with them in a natural, human way?

Finally, **these metaphors suggest an ideal destination rather than honoring each person's unique sense of belonging,** usually reducing the final stage to a label like 'donor' or 'major gift.'

But if someone isn't ready for those stages, is that relationship a failure? Is it a "lost opportunity?" Can we still see them as a valuable part of our mission? Of course, we would say they are. Yet do those individuals feel that following a prescribed path is the only way to belong?

What if individuals had a meaningful way to belong to our mission, regardless of their capacity, circumstances, or stage of involvement?

The reality is that we don't live in funnels, and we are not on a linear journey. **We live in dynamic, ever-changing human relationships.**

We live in relationships with the world around us, with one another, and with causes we care about.

We linger.

We wander.

We lean in.

We take a step back.

We show up unexpectedly.

We stay quietly involved for years.

We hang around the fringes.

Then, suddenly, we are all in.

We jump in quickly.

Then, we need to step back.

In other words, we are **human.**

What if our engagement strategy reflected this nonlinear reality of belonging?

What if, instead of treating people like Honda Civics on an assembly line, we invited them into community, belonging, and partnership in ways that make sense for them and where they are in life?

What if we had a framework that built trust, celebrated individuality, and gave us a strategy for engaging people in an organic, human way?

What if we stopped thinking about funnels, journeys, and pipelines? What if we started thinking in terms of spaces?

CHAPTER 1

AN OVERVIEW OF THE FOUR SPACES

The Four Spaces of Nonprofit Engagement model is rooted in how humans are wired to belong and engage. It provides an effective communications and donor relations framework that meets people where they are.

It helps you know what to say… and when to say it.
This framework helps you evaluate who you're talking to and then discern the best way to engage them in a way that builds trust.

But this isn't just theory. It's a way of thinking, shaped by lived experience and grounded in human research.

We're not inventing something new here. This framework draws from Christopher Alexander and his theories on design and pattern language[1], which explore how physical spaces shape human connection. It is informed by Edward T. Hall's research on proxemics, the study of how people relate through physical distance[2]. And finally, it draws heavily on Joseph Myers' book *The Search to Belong*[3], which has significantly influenced this model.

Hall identified four zones of physical distance: public, social, personal, and intimate. Myers took this further, reframing these zones as relational spaces of belonging. His insight was that connection isn't merely about physical proximity; it's about how people experience belonging. This interpretive leap provides the foundation for the framework you're reading here.

Myers originally developed this model to help faith and community leaders understand how people belong differently across relational spaces. His work continues to inform organizational design far beyond religious contexts.

The Welcoming Nonprofit applies Myers' framework to the world of nonprofit communications, exploring how these same relational dynamics can guide donor engagement.

We're indebted to these thinkers as we develop a guide

---

[1]Christopher Alexander, *A Pattern Language: Towns, Buildings, Construction* (Oxford University Press, 1977).
[2]Edward T. Hall, *The Hidden Dimension* (Doubleday, 1966).
[3]Joseph R. Myers, *The Search to Belong: Rethinking Intimacy, Community, and Small Groups* (Zondervan, 2003).

for engaging people naturally.

This model is intuitive, flexible, and easy to use, mainly because it reflects the relational spaces we all move through.

Like any good model, it helps to have a visual that isn't linear or mechanical.

Anthropologist Edward T. Hall studied how people experience space in relationships.

He identified four distinct zones of belonging:

- **Public Space** – More than 12 feet apart
- **Social Space** – Roughly 4 to 12 feet apart
- **Personal Space** – About 1.5 to 4 feet apart
- **Intimate Space** – From 18 inches to actual contact

A Working Definition of Belonging:

Belonging is the confident awareness that I am seen, safe, and significant in this space, with the freedom to approach, remain, or step back. Without penalty.

Joe Myers made a key observation. He notes that in each of these four spaces:

- We connect

- We are committed, and we participate
- We find the connection significant

As he emphasizes in *The Search to Belong*, every space of belonging carries equal value. No one space is more valuable than another. Public and social spaces are just as important as personal and intimate ones, each offering real meaning in its own way.

How do we apply this idea to donor relations?

Let's start with a snapshot of how each space works:

Belonging isn't a straight line. People move between spaces in their own time, in their own way. Movement isn't linear. It's human.

The Sidewalk

Who's Here	What They Need	How We Connect	Messaging Focus	Invitation
Strangers: *Website visitors, social followers, friends of friends*	**Clarity:** *Curiosity, freedom from commitment*	**Informal:** *Website homepage, social media, ads, flyers*	**Simple:** *Big picture impact, mission, blog & social content*	**Inquire:** *Follow us, subscribe, share, download something free*

A quick but important clarification: these spaces describe how people experience connection, not the communication channels you use.

The Front Porch

Who's Here	What They Need	How We Connect	Messaging Focus	Invitation
Acquaintances: *First-time donors, subscribers, event attendees*	**Connection:** *Trust, feeling seen & welcomed*	**Casual:** *Newsletters, welcome emails, intro events*	**Inspiring:** *Impact stories, stats, team introductions*	**Follow:** *Give again, attend something, sign up, meet someone*

The Living Room

Who's Here	What They Need	How We Connect	Messaging Focus	Invitation
Friends: *Recurring donors, volunteers, advocates*	**Belonging:** *Relationship, emotional investment*	**Personal:** *Tours, behind-the-scenes, calls, thank-you notes*	**Sincere:** *Vision updates, real stories, program depth*	**Engage:** *Volunteer leadership, recurring giving, closer connection*

The Kitchen Table

Who's Here	What They Need	How We Connect	Messaging Focus	Invitation
Partners: *Board members, major donors, staff, legacy givers*	**Ownership:** *Transparency, influence*	**Familial:** *1:1 meetings, dinners, strategic gatherings*	**Honest:** *Financials, challenges, long-term vision*	**Co-create:** *Major gifts, co-creation, legacy commitments*

The same email can feel like waving to a stranger on the Sidewalk or a meaningful conversation in the Living Room, depending on trust, tone, and history. A board meeting can feel like the Kitchen Table for one member and the Front Porch for another who's still finding their footing.

Channels are tools. Spaces are felt.

This matters because it keeps us from falling into a common trap: assuming that switching platforms or tactics will automatically deepen relationships. It won't. What deepens relationships is meeting people where they actually are, not where our org chart says they should be.

As you read the chapters ahead, hold this tension lightly. We'll talk about channels and tactics because you need

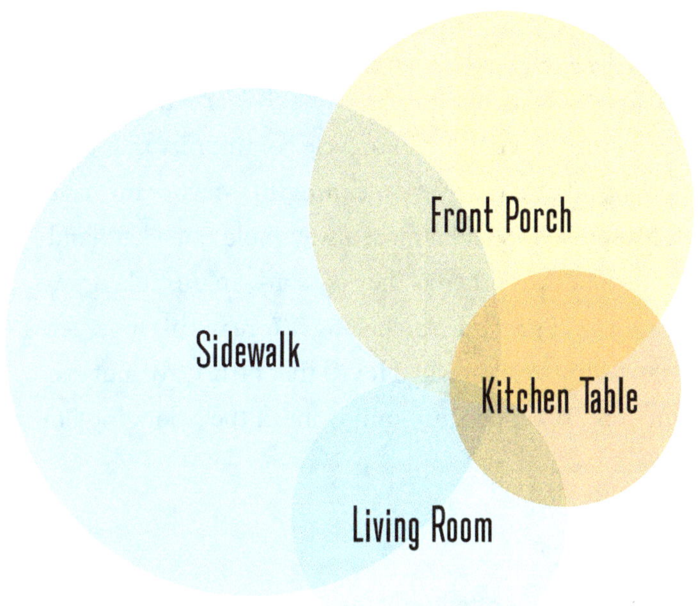

practical ways to apply this. But the real work is learning to read the relational temperature of each person and adjust your posture accordingly.

Now, let's explore each space in more detail so you can recognize them, nurture them intentionally, and communicate with clarity and trust.

Let's think about what these spaces look like in everyday life:

Public Space

Back in the day, when I was young, hip, and cool, I started riding a motorcycle. I quickly learned that there is a connection in the motorcycle community that is very public and also feels very meaningful. Maybe you've seen it. Motorcyclists will almost always hold out a left hand to wave to each other as they pass. It's an unspoken way of saying, "I see you. You belong. We're in this together." I can't fully explain why I loved that little wave, but every time I see it happen, it reminds me of the belonging I once felt.

Social Space

The people you often only see in social settings fall into this category: work friends, teammates, or those who share a club or hobby. Conversations here are usually small talk, and they don't have to be profound to matter. In these moments, we share small but important parts of our lives. We begin to discern whether to hold people at a distance or move closer and explore the possibility of a deeper connection. Far from being just a transition, this space is meaningful in its own right.

Personal Space

Personal space is where the conversation moves below the surface. It's where we tell stories, share feelings, and laugh or cry together. Here we share aspects of our lives that go beyond what we would share in a social media post. That is because we share this space with close friends and family.

Intimate Space

Your closest connections occupy this space: your partner, family, and lifelong friends. They are the ones who know your true self. In this space, you can be "naked" (figuratively, sometimes literally) and be fully accepted.

Too often, we treat personal and intimate spaces as the only ones that *really* matter. But the truth is, public, social, and personal spaces are just as vital to being whole, connected humans.

With that in mind, we offer a metaphor of a house situated in a neighborhood to bring this concept to life for your nonprofit:

- **Public Space** → *The Sidewalk*
- **Social Space** → *The Front Porch*
- **Personal Space** → *The Living Room*
- **Intimate Space** → *The Kitchen Table*

And your job as a nonprofit leader?

It's not to pressure people further into the house but to create spaces so inviting that they naturally want to spend more time there.

Let's explore what that looks like in practice.

CHAPTER 2

THE SIDEWALK: THE ART OF FIRST IMPRESSIONS

This is the space of first impressions, where strangers encounter your work for the first time and decide if it's worth a closer look.

I was in San Francisco recently and stopped by my favorite clothing store. The shop is one of the few places that carries what I believe is the greatest hoodie ever made, so I took the opportunity to replace my old, worn hoodie with a new one.

At the checkout, the cashier asked why I was in town, and I responded politely, with a surface-level response: "I'm here for work."

I didn't expect it, but he pressed a little: "What kind of work?"

I gave him my Sidewalk Statement: "I lead a branding

agency for nonprofits."

This has become my go-to answer when I meet strangers who ask what kind of work I do. Ninety-nine percent of the time, the response is the same: "Cool," and then we both move on.

But this time was different. This guy told me he was on the board of a local nonprofit, and the conversation naturally went deeper. It went from casual interest to questions about the kinds of organizations we work with and the kind of problems they are trying to solve.

We've all heard of the elevator pitch. But the Sidewalk Statement, or in this case, the checkout-counter pitch, can often be more useful. We usually do not have a 20-story elevator ride to talk about our work. In these situations, we have 3-5 seconds to answer the question in a clear, concise, and maybe even compelling way.

We have the opportunity to share just enough information with the other person so they can decide whether to continue the conversation or move on.

And either option is okay.

This approach honors the person in front of you. It doesn't automatically assume they're interested in what you're talking about. Assuming someone wants to hear all the details about your work just because you're passionate about it can be presumptuous and come across as self-centered.

A more generous approach is to share a clear, straightforward explanation of what you do while allowing people to decide whether to continue the conversation.

Unlike an elevator pitch, which gives you 30–60 seconds, a Sidewalk Statement might only last a few seconds. It offers enough clarity to spark curiosity, but doesn't require anything more than the moment allows. It doesn't require someone to be stuck with you in a claustrophobic metal box while you stop at each floor because some random kid pushed every button on the wall.

We have all heard the phrase, "You only get one chance to make a first impression."

Research shows we form opinions in milliseconds. Once these first impressions take hold, they're surprisingly resistant to change. If that first impression is positive, trust builds easily. If it's negative, you're fighting an uphill battle.

This is why your homepage, your sidewalk pitch, and your first email matter so much.

A Sidewalk Statement applies perfectly to nonprofit communications, especially to the "above-the-fold" section on your website's homepage. This is the first thing people see on their computer or phone screen before scrolling further or closing the tab.

We think of this vital real estate as your digital sidewalk. And you only have a few seconds to grab people's attention before they move on.

When someone lands on your site, you have about three to five seconds to create a compelling case for people to continue to scroll so they can learn more.

If that first impression feels bland, unclear, or overly complex, people will leave. Not because they don't care, but because it's too hard to grasp quickly amid everything else competing for their attention.

We all know attention spans are shrinking, inboxes are overflowing, and our collective bandwidth feels maxed out. The world around us is louder and more intense, and things are moving faster than ever.

When someone finds your organization, a simple, clear

The Sidewalk

Who's Here	What They Need	How We Connect	Messaging Focus	Invitation
Strangers: *Website visitors, social followers, friends of friends*	**Clarity:** *Curiosity, freedom from commitment*	**Informal:** *Website homepage, social media, ads, flyers*	**Simple:** *Big picture impact, mission, blog & social content*	**Inquire:** *Follow us, subscribe, share, download something free*

statement is not just good branding. It's an act of hospitality.

Let's take a look at what "Sidewalk" engagement looks like:

Who Is on the Sidewalk?

The folks you meet on the sidewalk are becoming aware of your organization for the first time. They might be acquaintances you meet in public, someone who saw a flyer, or the friend of a supporter. They might be checking out your website or browsing your Instagram feed.

They're not deeply engaged; they're simply investigating.

The sidewalk is all about first impressions, and, in this space, your message must be short, clear, and thoughtful.

What Do People Need on the Sidewalk?

When you encounter people on the sidewalk, they need clarity, not complexity. They aren't prepared to process your acronyms and insider language unique to the field you work in, nor are they equipped with years of research and understanding.

They simply want to know what you do and why it matters.

This reminds me of what I experience where I live in Portland, Oregon, where it's common for cashiers to ask,

"What are you up to today?"

I lived on the East Coast for 18 years, and I can't imagine anyone asking that question in a city like Philadelphia. The first time I heard that question in Portland, I remember thinking, "Why would you ask me that? Are you going to follow me home to rob me?"

Was my reaction dramatic? Yes. But that's kinda what happens when you live in Philly for 18 years.

It's a friendly question, but it's a bit too much, too fast for someone you've just met. Nobody wants to unpack their life story in the checkout line.

Yet nonprofits often make this mistake. We meet someone new and immediately launch into a three-minute monologue about our organizational history, mission, unique model, and details from our latest impact report.

It's just too much, too soon.

What people need on the sidewalk helps them decide: *Is this cause worth more of my attention?*

As a nonprofit leader, your job in sidewalk spaces is not to dump the complexity of your work onto the people you meet. It's your role to own the complexity… and offer clarity instead.

Your organization is solving some of the world's most challenging problems. Problems such as poverty, injustice, racism, education inequalities, public health crises, violence, or climate change.

That kind of work is incredibly nuanced and complex.

But when you jump right into all the complexities of your work, you risk losing people who would otherwise genuinely care, simply because you've overwhelmed them before you've earned their trust.

I am not suggesting that you dumb down your work to the extent that it loses its depth.

Instead, the challenge is to make it clear without over-simplifying, to create room for curiosity, and to invite people to engage at their own pace. The goal is to make it so clear and compelling that the people naturally want to learn more.

How Do We Connect on the Sidewalk?

The Sidewalk is a public space. It's where you share informal snapshots of your work: a homepage headline, a flyer placed on a bulletin board, a quote on Instagram, a brief mention in a conversation.

In these moments, your job is not to explain everything. It's to provide practical, simple on-ramps. It's an opportunity to say just enough so someone can ask for more information if they want.

When I taught my kids to drive, we started driving in

an empty parking lot. Then we moved to the side streets. Eventually, they made it onto the highway.

Too many nonprofits throw people straight into the passing lane in rush-hour traffic on the highway in their first interaction.

When creating space for people, it's important to start simple, build trust, and create a clear pathway toward meaningful engagement.

When you do that, you're giving them an opportunity to belong.

What is the Messaging Focus on the Sidewalk?

We have already talked about how the sidewalk is the place for clarity, but it is also the space for simplicity.

It seems counterintuitive, but it is challenging to keep things simple.

"If I had more time, I would have written a shorter letter."

— Blaise Pascal

It's one thing to deliver something short; it's another to provide something that's not only short, but simple and meaningful.

When we choose simplicity on the sidewalk, our message becomes:

- Easier to remember and recall
- Quicker to understand

- Stronger in its emotional impact
- Easier for others to share

Simplicity is challenging because, far too often, we are too close to our own ideas to know what is really important to others.

We can easily forget what it is like not to know all the details and assume that everyone knows as much as we do. As a result, we try to prove the value of our work by overexplaining rather than sharing just enough information to help people understand.

Simplicity is also tricky because including as much information as possible can create an unnecessarily heavy weight of responsibility. For some leaders, this tendency may be rooted in insecurity about how their work will be perceived.

The most confident communicators are often those who use fewer words. This is because they have done the hard work of distilling their message down to a few simple statements.

We have all been in situations where someone shared something about themselves or their work and overexplained it to the point that it seemed they either didn't know what they were talking about or, at the very least, weren't confident in what they were trying to say.

Leaders of complex organizations often have advanced

degrees. One downside of this, at least when it comes to communications, is that we can confuse complexity with intelligence. Long sentences, acronyms, or lofty mission statements might seem like they elevate your work, but they can create more confusion instead of clarity.

True clarity requires humility. It means translating big ideas into concepts that others can grasp quickly. This means leaders have to stop writing content and crafting messaging that will impress their peers and start communicating in ways that connect with the kind of people who can help move their mission forward.

As we'll see, there is a place for complexity, it's just not on the sidewalk.

What is the Invitation We Offer on the Sidewalk?

The key invitation on the sidewalk is simple: it's a call to inquire.

As The National Enquirer said in the '80s, "Inquiring minds want to know." On the sidewalk, we're looking for people who want to learn more about who we are, what we do, and how they can take the next step.

If curiosity is there, you need to offer ways to satisfy it. In marketing, this is about creating "calls to action" that fit the moment. In other words, the invitation should always match the level of connection someone is ready for.

For example, you wouldn't respond to someone who's simply inquiring about your work by explaining how to join the board of directors. That would be jarring, much like being asked what you are doing the rest of the day when you're just trying to buy coffee!

Instead, we should craft calls to action appropriate for the sidewalk space: join our mailing list, learn more, download a free resource, attend an upcoming event or webinar, or follow us on social media.

Whatever the invitation, it should encourage people to take one or two steps closer to your organization and join you on the Front Porch.

CHAPTER 3

THE FRONT PORCH: WHERE CURIOSITY TURNS INTO CONNECTION

This space is about welcoming, low-barrier connection. It's a place where people can linger without pressure, and begin to build trust.

When someone moves from the sidewalk to the front porch, it's not without risk. It's a vulnerable move. For a nonprofit leader, it might not feel like a significant risk to ask someone to sign up for an email, attend an event, take a phone call, meet for coffee, or make an initial donation.

But donors know that once they do that, they enter your space in a way that opens them up to the possibility of a relationship. And people don't enter these kinds of relationships lightly. When they do, they probably have expectations of what that relationship will look like.

When I first met Bill Cummings, my co-founder at Liminal, it was on a figurative front porch. We had never met before; we were simply attending the same conference. A mutual friend thought we might enjoy meeting one another and introduced us right before someone started speaking on the main stage.

After a brief, sidewalk-style conversation standing in the back of the room, we realized that we'd like to chat more and grabbed a seat in the back row of the conference room. Thankfully, the room was large; otherwise, it would have been more evident that we were completely ignoring the speaker. We talked, got to know each other, and realized we had quite a bit in common, and quickly learned that there was a lot we could talk about.

Our conversation lasted the entire session, which began a friendship that has lasted for more than 15 years. That initial meeting and front porch conversation (or, in this case, back-row-at-a-conference-venue conversation) led to a lifelong friendship.

Over the years, I have had plenty of conversations at conferences and many introductions from friends to people with shared interests. Some conversations stopped at the "sidewalk," otherwise known in that setting as a LinkedIn connection. Others moved to the Front Porch and stopped there. But a few have become much more significant, like when I met Bill.

This kind of connection is what the front porch is for.

It's an in-between space.

It's a space for what could become a more meaningful conversation.

It's not quite inside the house, but it's not entirely outside either.

It's the space where people decide to step into a more significant relationship or take another direction.

We only have so much capacity for personal relationships, and donors only have so much of their hearts (and resources) to go around. The front porch is essential for allowing people to opt in or out.

In the nonprofit world, the front porch is where someone first decides whether to invest in the relationship. They attend an event, subscribe to your newsletter, and give their first gift. It's not a deep commitment but a step towards a relationship.

This front porch is one of the most critical spaces and often gets overlooked.

We tend to focus heavily on acquiring strangers (the Sidewalk) and deepening relationships with people in the Living Room or at the Kitchen Table.

But the people on the front porch are right in the middle. They are within arm's reach because they are intrigued by what they have learned on the Sidewalk, but are not yet ready to make any long-term commitment. They've taken a step closer, sometimes tentatively.

How you respond to that "step closer" can make or break your relationship.

If you come on too strong, you risk scaring them off. If you don't provide more clarity about your work, you may miss the opportunity to engage them further.

If you have a solid plan to welcome them and give them space to understand your work more fully, you'll help them engage in ways that feel meaningful to them. More importantly, your hospitality will honor their time and respect their needs. By doing this, you establish trust, whether they decide to step into the living room or not.

Next, let's discuss what makes this space powerful and how to steward it well.

The Psychology of the Front Porch

Relationally, front porch spaces are built around casual warmth.

When I think of a front porch, I picture the beautiful Craftsman-style homes in North Portland. These neighborhoods were historically Black communities before systemic gentrification disrupted them. The homes still have big, welcoming porches with plenty of room for porch swings, tables, and chairs, where you can enjoy an ice-cold glass of lemonade. Once central to community life, these porches still carry a spirit of casual warmth.

These aren't the small front stoops you often find in suburban neighborhoods, where there is just enough space for a welcome mat and maybe a 'no soliciting' sign.

In suburban homes, the outdoor gathering spaces are in the back of the house on expansive decks with BBQs, cornhole, and strings of those big light bulbs you can get at Costco.

The back deck serves a very different purpose than the front porch.

While a back deck is a place for a family's inner circle of friends, where the conversation is more intimate and covers much more ground, the front porch is a place for light conversation and an opportunity to get to know each other more.

It's a transitional space that helps soften the line between our public and private lives. It's where new neighbors or friends can linger, conversations can happen without commitment, and we can lie to solicitors by telling them that our partner is not home, and we can't make a decision on solar panel installation or pest control without them.

In the language of anthropologist Edward T. Hall, this is the *social space*, where the distance between people is roughly four to 12 feet. That's close enough to talk without yelling, but far enough to keep some boundaries. It's the space of small talk, eye contact, light laughter, and nonverbal warmth.

In these moments, our minds are constantly buzzing with questions that help us determine if we're in a sincere and safe environment.

Can I trust this space? Do I feel welcomed here? Are the people here genuine, or just trying to sell me something?

Looking back on that first conversation with Bill, who was leading a nonprofit organization that worked in Guatemala, I remember asking similar questions.

Does this guy seem like a good leader? Is his nonprofit making a difference, or is it just doing something superficial? Can I trust him? Does he seem arrogant or humble? And most importantly, does he laugh at my jokes?

I am sure that in this front-porch/back-row conversation, he also asked some of the same questions about me.

Trust begins to grow in these casual, low-stakes conversations. And it's also where suspicions about motives, agendas, and integrity can be named, explored, and (hopefully) laid to rest.

For nonprofits, this means showing up like a good neighbor. Being warm, genuine, and willing to listen, all without assuming someone already wants to join us in the Living Room.

Our marketing, follow-ups, emails, and conversations should honor the front porch concept.

In this space, we are inviting without insisting and offering hospitality without pressure.

What "Front Porch" Engagement Looks Like

The Front Porch

Who's Here	What They Need	How We Connect	Messaging Focus	Invitation
Acquaintances: *First-time donors, subscribers, event attendees*	**Connection:** *Trust, feeling seen & welcomed*	**Casual:** *Newsletters, welcome emails, intro events*	**Inspiring:** *Impact stories, stats, team introductions*	**Follow:** *Give again, attend something, sign up, meet someone*

Who Is on the Front Porch?

The people on your front porch aren't strangers anymore, but they're not quite "in the house" either.

They've taken a meaningful step closer. They subscribed to your email list, attended your event, and maybe made their first small donation. They're saying, "I think I like what you're about, and I'd like to take another step to learn more."

They're not asking for the full story yet and don't want to feel pressured to do more, they do want to feel that the first step they take will *matter*.

People in this space are asking questions that they probably would not express out loud:

- Will anyone notice that I showed up?
- Will I be treated like a number?
- Will this feel human, or transactional?

How you answer matters. Your tone, follow-up, and messaging can determine whether they come back again or quietly slip away.

What Do People Need on the Front Porch?

The central need on the front porch is *connection*.

In this space, people are open. They're interested. But

they're also tentative.

What they want is to feel **seen.**

That means they are looking for:

- A warm, personal welcome (not a canned auto-response)
- An email that sounds like it came from a human
- A story that reminds them why your work matters
- A gentle acknowledgment of the step they just took

This isn't the time for heavy-handed asks or detailed reports.

This is the time to create relational momentum. A light and authentic rhythm that keeps the conversation going.

Think of it like being at a casual social event. Someone walks over to say "hi". You don't hand them a 12-page booklet about your life. You smile, introduce yourself, and ask a simple question. You make it easy to keep a conversation going.

How Do We Connect on the Front Porch?

We connect on the front porch with a friendly, personal, and low-pressure tone.

Some tools that are helpful in this space might include:

- Welcome email sequences that are warm and honest
- Stories that spotlight people, not just programs

- Handwritten thank-you notes for first-time donors
- An invitation to something casual and easy, like an open house or webinar

You're not trying to move them into the living room or kitchen just yet. You're just showing them that the front porch light is on, that someone is home, and that they matter.

And when the time is right, they are much more likely to take steps forward.

What Is the Messaging Focus on the Front Porch?

The tone on the front porch should be inspiring. The goal isn't to be flashy or to create an emotional connection using manipulation. No, instead the goal is to create a genuine picture of the good you're doing, and why it matters.

You want to help people imagine themselves as part of the story.

Connecting with people in this space might look like:

- Sharing a glimpse of real impact
- Introducing your team or values
- Painting a picture of what's possible

The goal here isn't to *inform* them to take action. It's to *inspire* them to stay connected.

What Is the Invitation on the Front Porch?

The call to action on the front porch is to *follow.*

Not in the social media sense (although that's great too). But in the relational sense.

You're inviting them to take one more step by:

- Making a second gift
- Attending a casual gathering
- Forwarding your email to a friend
- Asking a question
- Meeting with someone on your team

These are small, meaningful actions. They are actions people can take that convey, "I think I'll stick around a bit."

And your job is to make that choice easy.

Because when people feel seen and welcomed without pressure, they often choose to accept your invitation to join you in the Living Room.

CHAPTER 4

THE LIVING ROOM: THE POWER OF MAKING PEOPLE FEEL AT HOME

This is where deeper belonging begins to form. Conversations deepen, trust grows, and emotional investment takes root.

A man entered my living room without being invited. Let's just say it was an incredibly jarring experience.

He was big, shirtless, bleeding, and obviously, to me, high on drugs. Without our invitation or permission, he decided that our living room was the safest place to seek refuge from people pursuing him.

It's a long story, and this isn't the setting to share the full details. But, he was safely arrested after doing significant damage to our home, thankfully without anyone in my family being harmed.

At that moment, I learned firsthand that a living room is a sacred space—it's for invited guests, people we want to build something real with. We don't invite just anyone into our living rooms. The bug-sprayer guy, the solar salesman (I seem to be picking on him a lot), and the traveling encyclopedia salesman (do they still exist?!) can all stay on the front porch or maybe even the sidewalk.

But the people we invite into our living room are people we determine to be safe and worthy of getting to know more deeply. Similarly, those who find their way into your living room are looking to establish a different level of relationship.

> *"Every living room should be a place where people can sit down, feel at ease, and talk."*
> —Christopher Alexander, A Pattern Language

It is the living room where relationships begin to deepen. It's where you start to hear the more extensive version of someone's story, not just a headline and short blurb. In a living room, history is shared, trust takes root, and conversations move below the surface.

In this space, we learn the stories that have shaped them and how their journey has unfolded to bring them where they are. This is where you decide to wade into vulnerability and open your hearts towards the person you are hosting.

It's a casual, yet more intimate connection space.

Unlike the front porch, the living room invites you to stay longer, sit down, and open up. You're not yet at the kitchen table, where we'll learn that the most candid conversations happen, but we are beginning to move in that direction.

This is where belonging begins to really take shape. This happens through laughter, stories, and the small but significant choice to show up more fully.

What "Living Room" Engagement Looks Like

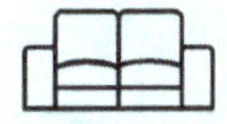

The Living Room

Who's Here	What They Need	How We Connect	Messaging Focus	Invitation
Friends: *Recurring donors, volunteers, advocates*	**Belonging:** *Relationship, emotional investment*	**Personal:** *Tours, behind-the-scenes, calls, thank-you notes*	**Sincere:** *Vision updates, real stories, program depth*	**Engage:** *Volunteer leadership, recurring giving, closer connection*

Who Is in Your Living Room?

For nonprofit leaders, the living room is the space for those who have chosen to be connected and affiliated with your organization. These people are recurring donors, have attended more than one in-person event, actively volunteer with your work, or advocate for your mission with their networks.

These are the folks you might call close companions in the work. They are the heart and soul of your organization, the everyday supporters of your work.

These friends are no longer strangers. They have moved past the point of being casual acquaintances. They've crossed the threshold between the front porch and the inside of your home because something about your mission resonated with them. Maybe your mission connects to their personal story or a deeply held conviction in their hearts.

Those sitting with you around your coffee table are often recurring donors, faithful volunteers, and advocates who regularly show up and offer their skills and voice.

In the living room, people are emotionally invested. They've moved from being observers to engaged supporters. They want—and need—more comprehensive insight into your work. They've decided they're ready to continue building trust and to explore whether your values truly align with theirs. They're looking for confirmation that this is a place they can genuinely belong.

What Do People Need in the Living Room?

The felt need of someone visiting in the living room is very different from that of someone on the sidewalk or front porch. Those sitting with you in your living room seek belonging, a real relationship, personal investment, and emotional connection.

People are not looking for a polished, surface-level engagement in these living room spaces. They've already decided your mission is worth their attention, so the sales pitch should be over. At this point, they want a relationship.

Think about the difference between chatting with a neighbor on your front porch and settling into your living room. You might talk about the weather on the front porch or swap quick updates about kids' sports.

But once you cross the threshold between the outside and inside of the home, the conversation becomes more personal. You might share what's really going on at work, how your kids are doing in sports, and the hard lessons they are learning. You might share the story behind the photo on the wall. The space itself invites connection, which requires honesty.

It works the same way in nonprofit relationships. When people enter your living room, they're not looking for perfect PR or tightly spun narratives. That messaging is for the sidewalk and front porch. No, the folks in your living room are open to nuance. They want to hear a more authentic story. They are looking for honesty and hope and are open to learning about the challenges you are facing. They want to see the "real" nonprofit, not just the staged version.

Too often, nonprofits make the mistake of treating living room friends like sidewalk strangers. We send them glossy impact reports but never tell them the story of the hard decisions behind the numbers. We thank them for their generosity, but don't let them see how much their trust means when things are uncertain.

What people need in the living room is to know: Do I truly belong here? Do you trust me enough to be real with me? Can I see myself in this story? Am I not just a supporter, but also a friend?

As a leader, your job in living room spaces is not to impress but to invite, not to perform, but to connect. This is where trust grows, stories are shared, and people begin to feel a deeper sense of belonging.

How Do We Connect in the Living Room?

The Living Room is a personal space. It's where you slow

down, sit together, and share more than superficial updates.

There is a specific posture in the living room that is distinct from the other spaces. On the sidewalk, the posture might be arms crossed or slightly closed. On the front porch, we're sitting upright on wooden rocking chairs. In the living room, we sit back, settle into a comfortable chair or sofa, and relax.

We open ourselves up more to those in the living room. Sure, we're not fully open yet, that's for the kitchen table, but in the living room, we are more likely to let ourselves be seen.

Too often, nonprofits invite supporters inside their organizational living room, keeping them at arm's length, and treating them like strangers. We offer templated thank-you notes or glossy brochures when people want an authentic conversation and meaningful connection.

Living room connections happen through handwritten notes, phone calls, small-group gatherings, or behind-the-scenes updates that show the heart behind the numbers.

In other words, this is not the place for rehearsed speeches and elevator pitches. It is for listening as much as sharing, pulling back the curtain and letting people see both the wins and the challenges.

When you connect this way, you're giving people information and trust.

We all know that trust is the soil where true belonging grows.

What Is the Messaging Focus in the Living Room?

If it isn't clear already, the messaging focus in the living room is stories, stories, stories!

This is where we share stories of success, failures, and challenges. These stories should be inspirational and vulnerable.

The inspirational stories talk about the heroes of our organization (the community we serve!) finding success, redemption, and hope. The vulnerable stories we share are the nuances and challenges we face; they are the real-life, rubber-meets-the-road stories that invite people into the complexities of our work.

Since the living room is where stories are shared, it's the right place to introduce the idea of the hero. Much has been written about the hero's journey. This concept was popularized by American mythologist Joseph Campbell in his 1949 book *The Hero with a Thousand Faces*.

In that work, Campbell studied myths, legends, and stories from cultures across the world and identified a recurring narrative pattern he called the "monomyth." It's a universal structure in which every hero follows a similar path.

In Campbell's framework, the hero will:

1. Leave their ordinary world,

2. Face trials and challenges in an unfamiliar one,

3. Transform through the struggle, and

4. Returns with new wisdom, gifts, or power to benefit their community.

This cycle became known as the Hero's Journey. While the idea wasn't entirely new, Campbell popularized it as a storytelling framework, drawing heavily on earlier work by anthropologist Arnold van Gennep (*Rites of Passage*, 1909) and psychologist Carl Jung, who explored archetypes and the collective unconscious.

Later, in the 1970s–80s, filmmaker George Lucas explicitly credited Campbell's work as the inspiration for Star Wars, which launched the Hero's Journey into mainstream storytelling, marketing, and leadership theory.

In recent years, Donald Miller established the Story-Brand[4] framework, which is built on the idea that every

---

[4] Donald Miller, *Building a StoryBrand: Clarify Your Message So Customers Will Listen* (Nashville: HarperCollins Leadership, 2017).

hero's journey follows a seven-step narrative.

1. A character,

2. Has a problem,

3. And meets a guide,

4. Who gives them a plan

5. And calls them to action

6. That helps them avoid failure

7. And ends in success.

Miller rightfully points out that once you learn this formula, it changes how you experience movies, stories, and marketing.

In nonprofit storytelling, we have a unique challenge and temptation.

Often, nonprofits are tempted to make donors the heroes of the story. But that model is unhealthy and incomplete. Donors may love being cast as the hero of their own story, or worse, of someone else's. But when we frame nonprofit storytelling this way, it misdirects the work and de-centers the very people being served. Instead, it places privilege at the center. And in doing so, we miss the chance to tell a more honest and compelling story: that the people and communities we serve are the true heroes of their own stories.

In the nonprofit hero's journey, we need to think of the donor and the nonprofit organization as guides. When we do this, we ensure that those served by nonprofits remain at the center and that the work does not become a self-absorbed endeavor for the organization or the donor.

Thinking back to the hero's journey and Storybrand frame work, the nonprofit leader and the donor are Yoda, and the person being served by your nonprofit is Luke Skywalker.

So, in the living room, let's tell stories, inviting donors to come alongside you to guide someone else's epic story, where we call them to action and help their communities avoid failure and move toward success.

What Is the Invitation in the Living Room?

The invitation in the living room is to engage more fully, to settle in, and "join us."

The people sitting with us have already crossed the threshold. They are donors, maybe recurring donors, volunteers, and advocates who want to stay connected.

The next step is to invite them into greater participation. This might look like a new volunteer leadership role, shifting from one-time giving to recurring giving, or joining a conversation where their voice helps shape the work.

For others, it could mean raising funds on their birthday, visiting the community being served, or mentoring a program participant or staff member. The possibilities are wide open for anyone moved by your story.

It's important to note that these aren't merely transactional asks. They're relational invitations and calls to belonging. They're relational invitations and calls to belonging. The invitation should convey, "You belong here, and we'd love for you to bring even more of yourself into this space."

The goal is not to pressure, but to affirm: "You're already part of the story. Here's a way to step further in."

CHAPTER 5

THE KITCHEN TABLE: WHERE TRUST BECOMES PARTNERSHIP

The most intimate space in the nonprofit organization, where people are invited to contribute, lead, and shape the future alongside you.

Growing up, I lived just a few blocks away from my best friend. This, of course, was the era of growing up without cell phones, where you would go over to your friend's house and say, "Can Chad come out and play?" Then you'd disappear into the neighborhood for hours on your BMX bike, and your parents would have to be reminded they had kids as they watched the 10 o'clock news. And yes, kids, that was an actual thing.

My aforementioned friend Chad had "back door rights." This is the next step after "fridge rights." This meant that when he came over, he wouldn't knock to ask if I was home; he would just come in the back door without knocking. If I wasn't home? That really didn't matter. He'd generally make himself comfortable until I was.

In fact, it wasn't abnormal for our family to come back home and find Chad in our house, eating cereal at our Kitchen Table. We didn't think twice about it. It's not as if we were surprised by an intruder at our table, eating a bowl of porridge. Instead, it seemed perfectly normal!

My relationship with Chad was such that coming home to find him eating our cereal at our Kitchen Table was not only okay, but it was honoring. There was something beautiful about that level of relationship where Chad knew that he had a place at our table, even when we weren't home.

That's the kind of trust we're talking about in this space. The folks at the Kitchen Table aren't intruders; they are partners who know they belong at the table, whether you're expecting them or not. They are the ones who drop in unexpectedly, and they are always welcome.

It's at the Kitchen Table where we move from familiarity to shared ownership. We move from nuance to vulnerability and transparency. At these tables, papers are strewn out in front of you as you analyze budgets and long-range plans. At the nonprofit Kitchen Table, we are joined by our closest partners, staff members, board members, and most engaged volunteers.

What Kitchen Table Engagement Looks Like:

The Kitchen Table

Who's Here	What They Need	How We Connect	Messaging Focus	Invitation
Partners: *Board members, major donors, staff, legacy givers*	**Ownership:** *Transparency, influence*	**Familial:** *1:1 meetings, dinners, strategic gatherings*	**Honest:** *Financials, challenges, long-term vision*	**Co-create:** *Major gifts, co-creation, legacy commitments*

Who Is at the Kitchen Table?

Think about it; you don't invite just anyone to sit with you at your kitchen table. It's just too intimate a spot. We're not standing on guard like on the sidewalk, or sitting upright on the front porch, or sitting back more relaxed in the living room.

The people at your Kitchen Table have a different posture: they are leaning in. These partners are sitting on the edge of their seats with a personal, vested interest in the work. They are lending their expertise. They take the time to review financial reports, pore over strategic plans, and ask tough questions. When we are at the Kitchen Table, we are sitting with those who will not only support the future but also help *shape* it.

This is a familial space. It's not family (that's an overused and unhelpful metaphor), but it is familial. It's as close to family as one can get to being part of your organization's mission.

What Do People Need at the Kitchen Table?

When people sit with us at the kitchen table, they need transparency and vulnerability, which leads to the deepest levels of trust.

Far too often, leaders hold their cards too close to the vest. We are slow to share our struggles, fears, worries, or anxiety. In some spaces, that is actually a good thing! You do not want to share the most profound complexities of your leadership and organization with people on the sidewalk, the front porch, or even the living room.

These topics need to be reserved for the Kitchen Table. With papers strewn all about, sometimes with your head in your hands or your fist on the table, this is the environment of wrestling with what's next, what's gone wrong, and what's gone well. It's not that we are dishonest in the other spaces; it is just that the Kitchen Table is the context where people are ready for complex conversations.

If the Sidewalk is the space of simplicity and clarity, the Kitchen Table is the space of complexity and candor. And the people at the table need that from you if they are going to engage fully.

They didn't pull up a chair to your Kitchen Table to get bite-sized tweets and tidbits. They sat down for depth. If they are going to help you create the future, you need to let them in.

How Do We Connect at the Kitchen Table?

Since the Kitchen Table is a familial space, conversations slow, voices are lowered, and real decisions are made. Connection in this space isn't about inspiration, like in the living room; it's about intimacy and shared responsibility.

Think about your own kitchen table. It's where the family budget gets discussed, tough choices about jobs or schooling are weighed, and future plans are sketched on the back of an envelope. It's not always tidy, but it's where the most important conversations happen because everyone knows their voice matters.

In the nonprofit world, connecting at the Kitchen Table means creating space for that same kind of candor. It looks like one-on-one meetings, strategy dinners, financial transparency, or small gatherings where you put real challenges on the table. It's about asking for input, not just reporting outcomes.

Too many organizations either avoid these conversations

because they fear vulnerability or rush into them before trust is earned. But when done well, the Kitchen Table becomes a place where your closest partners don't just support your mission, they help shape it.

The Three Guardrails of Intimacy, a Few Principles that Help Keep this Space Healthy:

1. **Consent:** invite, don't presume.

2. **Transparency:** share risks and tradeoffs, not just outputs.

3. **Reciprocity:** talk *with* people, not *at* them; co-author the future.

What Is the Messaging Focus at the Kitchen Table?

The tone at the kitchen table is honest.

This is where you put away the slides and soundbites and speak plainly. It's where you share financial realities, acknowledge tradeoffs, and name the challenges ahead. The people at your table aren't here for the polished version; they want the whole picture, even if it's complicated.

Kitchen table messaging should blend candor with vision. Partners in this space don't just want to hear what's hard; they also want to hear where you're headed and why the risk is worth it. They're not scared off by complexity. In fact, they respect it when you trust them enough to carry the complexity with you.

Think about sitting with a major donor who is about to invest $100,000 in your work. What are they looking for? Are they looking only for platitudes and good stories? Sure, that may be what drew them in at first, but before making a significant gift, they will want to understand your plans, the details, the complexities, and exactly how their investment will change lives in concrete ways.

What Is the Invitation at the Kitchen Table?

In the nonprofit space, we often use the term "co-creation." This concept is borrowed from design, business, and other sectors, but it takes on unique significance at the kitchen table because this is ground zero for shared ownership of the mission.

Again, when we are at the table with our key partners, board members, and major donors to invest and co-create, it's a call to roll up our sleeves, get into the mess and complexity, and get to work.

Major donors and partners aren't interested in signing up for a mailing list; hopefully, they've already done that. Major donors aren't sitting at your table to be asked to give $10/month; they have more capacity than that.

Major donors, partners, and board members want to know how to help you solve your most significant challenges. Failing to invite them into that work undervalues the seat they've chosen to occupy at the table. Their presence signals trust, capacity, and commitment. To treat them like casual supporters is to undervalue both the relationship and the difference they're ready to make.

CHAPTER 6

THE POSTURES BEHIND THE PRACTICE

Three Mindset Shifts Before You Begin

Before you start mapping your communications to the Four Spaces, there are a few important clarifications we need to note.

1. Channels ≠ Spaces

Earlier, we said that channels are tools and spaces are felt. Here's how to put that into practice.

The channel doesn't determine the space. The person's experience does.

A handwritten note can serve as a Kitchen Table interaction or a Sidewalk touchpoint, depending on whether it comes across as personal or templated. A one-on-one meeting can remain a Front Porch if trust hasn't been established yet.

So how do you know which space someone is actually experiencing? Ask yourself these four questions:

1.   **How personal is the content?** Is this message specific to them, or could it be applied to anyone?

2.   **Is there mutual visibility?** Do they feel known, and do you truly know them? Or is this a one-way broadcast?

3.   **What's the expectation of a reply?** Does this message open a dialogue, or is it intended as a one-way update?

4.   **How much trust already exists?** Have you earned the right to this level of access, or are you simply assuming it?

Your answers to these questions won't provide you with a formula, but they'll help you assess whether your message matches the relational space you think you're in.

2. Concentric & Overlapping Belonging

Now remember, your organization isn't the only one they're part of.

The people connected to your mission also belong to families, churches, neighborhood groups, professional associations, alumni networks, and other causes they care about. Each of these communities has its own Sidewalk, Front Porch, Living Room, and Kitchen Table. And your donors are occupying different spaces in each one. It's easy to assume our cause is the only one that truly matters to them, but it rarely is.

Consider our imaginary friend, Sarah. She's a recurring donor to your organization, which might put her in your Living Room. But she's also:

- At the Kitchen Table with her extended family, helping manage her aging parents' care
- In the Living Room at her church, where she serves on a committee
- On the Front Porch with a climate justice nonprofit she started following last year
- On the Sidewalk with her college alumni association, skimming their emails but rarely engaging

Sarah has a *finite* amount of relational and financial capacity. She can't be at every Kitchen Table. No one can.

What this means for you:

When someone stays on your Front Porch for years, it doesn't always mean you failed to make them feel welcome, or that your messaging was off. It might simply mean that their Kitchen Tables are already full.

This isn't cause for despair. It's a cause for humility and patience.

Your job isn't to compete for closer access. It's to be a good steward of the space they've chosen, trusting that if and when their capacity opens up, they'll know they're welcome to move closer.

A few practical implications:

1. **Ask better questions.** When you get to know donors, learn about their other commitments. Not to size up the competition, but to understand their lives.

2. **Celebrate the space they're in.** If someone has been a faithful Front Porch friend for five years, that's not a stuck relationship. That's a sustained one.

3. **Time your invitations wisely.** Major life transitions often shift capacity. Kids leave home. Careers wind down. Loved ones pass. These moments can open space for a more grounded sense of belonging, but only if you've been a patient, trustworthy, welcoming presence all along.

4. **Release the pressure.** When you understand that people are managing multiple belongings, you stop interpreting distance as rejection. It frees you to show up with openness without keeping score.

The goal of this framework isn't to pull everyone into your Kitchen. It's to create spaces so welcoming that people know where they stand and feel valued wherever they are.

With those lenses in place, here are some practical ways to move forward.

3. Choice as Hospitality

Here's a counterintuitive truth: the easier you make it to leave, the more likely people are to stay.

Real hospitality doesn't trap people. It invites them. A genuine invitation always includes the freedom to decline.

Think about the best dinner parties you've attended. The host didn't block the door or guilt you for leaving early. They welcomed you warmly, made you feel at home, and trusted you to decide when it was time to go. That freedom is what made you want to go back.

Nonprofits often get this backwards. We hide unsubscribe links. We send guilt-laden emails to lapsed donors. We treat someone stepping away—whether from a mailing list, a recurring gift, or an event—as a failure to prevent rather than a decision to respect.

But when people sense they can't easily step back in, something shifts. The relationship stops feeling like hospitality and starts feeling manipulative. Trust erodes. What could have been a pause becomes a permanent goodbye.

What choice looks like in each space:

- **On the Sidewalk:** Make it clear what they're signing up for. No bait-and-switch. If they give you their email, let them know what to expect and how often they'll hear from you.

- **On the Front Porch:** Honor the pace they set. If someone attends one event and disappears for six months, welcome them back without commentary when they return.

- **In the Living Room:** Create space for people to step back without shame. Life changes. Capacity shifts. A recurring donor who needs to pause isn't a lost cause; they're a person navigating real constraints.

- **At the Kitchen Table:** Even your closest partners need permission to set boundaries. Board members burn out. Major donors face family crises. The intimacy of this space is preserved when people know they can be honest about their limits.

Permission. Reversibility. Easy exits. These aren't signs of shallow commitment. They're the foundation of trust.

When people know they're free to go, they're also free to

stay for the right reasons.

One more thing: these spaces aren't experienced the same way by everyone. A person's cultural context shapes how proximity and disclosure are perceived. What feels warm and welcoming in one context might feel intrusive or cold in another. Neurodivergent individuals may experience sensory environments and social cues very differently from you. Power dynamics matter too. A first-generation donor may feel the weight of your institutional space in ways a legacy philanthropist never will. Stay curious. Pay attention to cues. And don't assume your experience is the norm.

CHAPTER 7

CRAFTING A SIDEWALK STATEMENT

Giving People the Freedom to Lean In or Move On

One of the most practical things you can take away from this book is what we call *The Sidewalk Statement*.

This might sound like marketing heresy, but the elevator pitch is not a good starting point for explaining what your organization does. I know it's been treated like it for decades, but in the world we live in today, it's not.

It's too much, too soon, at least for most first conversations. No one really wants to talk to a stranger for that long, at least not without a way to get out of the conversation (which is what makes elevators so awful; there is no way out). And honestly, no one wants to talk to *anyone* in an elevator. It's beyond me why we chose one of the most awkward places for conversation as the metaphor for explaining our organization's focus.

Speaking of awkward, a friend of mine found a way to make being in an elevator with strangers even more un-comfortable than it already is. When we would be on an elevator full of people, he would wait until just before we reached our floor, and would turn around, face everyone with his back to the door, and, like a social experiment gone wrong, he would say, "So what do you guys want to talk about?"

He would time it so that just as he finished the question, the doors would open, and he would say, "Aw man, this is our floor, great meeting you all!"

I loved looking back as people's faces showed a mix of surprise, horror, and discomfort at the idea of having an actual conversation with a stranger in an elevator. So yeah, I feel like there is room for a different kind of initial conversation with a stranger, one that starts in a better meeting place than a cramped, claustrophobic elevator. The Sidewalk.

If I'm being fair, I'll admit the elevator pitch isn't fully dead. It's just been miscast. It's more of a front-porch conversation, and it's actually not a terrible one. As my son's baseball coach exclaims when his players put in good effort but get bad results, "I don't hate it!" It just doesn't belong on the sidewalk or in the first meeting.

Remember my cashier friend in San Francisco? My Sidewalk Statement was simple: "I lead a branding agency for nonprofits." That was enough for him to decide that he wanted to know more. He continued the conversation on his own, telling me he was on the board of a local nonprofit, and from there, it opened up naturally. That conversation led to an elevator pitch. It just earned its way into the moment instead of being forced on someone who never asked for it. Just the thought of that makes me want to take the stairs.

In an attention economy, a Sidewalk Statement is much more useful than an elevator pitch. It is short, easy to remember, and simple enough that anyone can understand it the first time they hear it.

So let's get into what a Sidewalk Statement looks like. It's a one-sentence identity statement that answers the question, "So, what does your organization do?" At its core, it follows a simple format: We are a nonprofit organization that [what you do].

It is just one sentence under 15 words that can be spoken in plain, conversational English.

And here's the key: it should be something you rehearse that doesn't sound rehearsed. People know instinctively when they're hearing something that's been memorized. It's just obvious and almost as awkward as those elevator rides.

This might go against everything your high school speech teacher taught you, but you will know you have a good Sidewalk Statement when you can drop in normal speech patterns like "oh," "well," and even "um," and it still feels natural. A good Sidewalk Statement should feel natural when it's spoken aloud. You shouldn't have to rehearse it or read it from an old-school index card. If it feels scripted when you say it, it's not ready yet.

You should not think of this statement as a hook, a way to reel people in so you can convert them into being recurring donors or future board members.

Instead, the Sidewalk Statement should serve more as a filter. It should be interesting enough to cause the right people lean in and ask more questions, and clear enough to let the wrong people politely move on. Both outcomes should be seen as a win.

Think back to the San Francisco clothing store from Chapter 2. My Sidewalk Statement, "I lead a branding agency for nonprofits," wasn't an attempt to impress or persuade the cashier. I wasn't in sales mode when I was simply there to buy my favorite hoodie. I just gave him enough information to decide whether to keep the conversation going. In that situation, he did. But the reality is, most people don't and won't. And, at the risk of being repetitive, that's *fine.*

I often find myself standing around with other parents

at my kids' baseball practices and games. When we run out of umpire calls to complain about, the conversation moves to things like "What do you do for work?"

In situations like that, I use my "branding agency for nonprofits" line all the time. Usually, the person I'm talking to says, "Huh, that's cool," and they move on. I have come to believe that kind of response is actually helpful. It lets me know that they don't really care about nonprofit branding, and that's okay.

But every once in a while, I meet someone who is on the board of a nonprofit, or works for one, or cares deeply about a specific nonprofit cause. Then, the conversation usually continues. In fact, some of our best baseball-parent friends are directly involved in nonprofit work. As I look back, what started as a sidewalk conversation eventually led to my wife working for a nonprofit we learned about at our son's baseball game — and ultimately to the Kitchen Table.

Start With What You Already Say

Before you start workshopping your new Sidewalk Statement, try this: write down what you currently say when someone at a coffee shop or a party asks, "What does your organization do?"

Don't clean it up or edit it. Just write it the way you actually say it. Or, better yet, grab one of your coworkers and ask them to answer that same question, and write down exactly what they say. In a situation like this, it might reveal much more than listening to yourself talk.

This exercise will likely reveal some common patterns. You might notice that your answer is way too long, too full of jargon or acronyms. It might be too focused on the mechanics of your work rather than the impact your organization actually has on your community. You might notice you've been giving a different answer every time because you've never really settled on one. If you're lucky, you will discover that your current answer is actually pretty close; it may just need some refining.

Whatever you find, starting with what you *already say* will give you a good place to start and something to work with. That will prove to be much easier than staring at a blank page.

Why This Is Harder Than It Sounds

Most nonprofit leaders I work with can talk about their organization for an hour without taking a breath. Often, I feel like I'm getting a doctoral-level seminar in trauma-informed, community-centric, intersectional systems change. You've probably used some of that terminology in a grant application recently, but they are words that do not belong on the sidewalk. So, I imagine that asking you to capture your work in one sentence is an entirely different challenge.

The unique challenge is that you probably know too much about your work to connect with people who know next to nothing about it. You are so close to the work that it's hard for you to talk about it in terms that people can relate to. Most nonprofit leaders I know are experts in a particular field and have a PhD-level of knowledge (often an actual PhD) about "trauma-informed, community-centric, intersectional systems change."

You know the history, the nuance, the complexity, the programs, the outcomes, and the stories behind the stories in your community and the difference you're trying to make. All of that knowledge and vital expertise make it incredibly hard to choose what to leave out. It can feel like you're oversimplifying your work or doing a disservice to the people you serve.

But remember what we talked about in Chapter 2: your job on the sidewalk is not to dump the complexity of your work into the laps of the people you meet. It's about owning the complexity and offering clarity instead.

It's easier when you realize that a Sidewalk Statement isn't the whole story. It's simply the beginning of the conversation. And yes, sometimes it is also the end of a conversation. But remember, both results are okay. Giving someone the clarity they need to decide whether to lean in or move on is one of the most generous things you can do.

That's hospitality. That's what it means to be, dare I say it, *The Welcoming Nonprofit*.

The Principles

Now, let's get down to some really practical tips when thinking about crafting a strong Sidewalk Statement.

You can follow simple principles:

Keep It Short

One sentence. Aim for 15 words or fewer. If you absolutely must, 20 max, but you will start getting into muddy water — and we all know muddy water definitely isn't clear. Anything longer and you're creeping into the kind of complexity that belongs on the front porch, not the sidewalk. Think of it this way: if you can't say it in one breath, it's too long.

Use Plain, Conversational Language

Remember: no acronyms allowed. No one knows what MTBESC means. By the way, I made that one up. If you recognized it, it wasn't a direct attack—but my point may have been made for at least one reader. Also, no obscure insider jargon, no boardroom language. And, it absolutely does not start with, "We exist to…".

The exception is when a technical term is actually the

clearest way to describe what you do. "Branding agency" is technically industry language, but most people understand it immediately. In cases like that, the jargon isn't confusing. Instead, it's efficient.

One organization we work with landed on this as their Sidewalk Statement: "*We are a nonprofit that integrates relational neuroscience and spiritual formation.*"

Does everyone know what *relational neuroscience* means? No. But they know it has something to do with the brain, and it's interesting enough to make the right person ask, "Wait, what does that mean?" Which is exactly what a Sidewalk Statement should do.

The jargon isn't clarifying in this case. It's intriguing. And intrigue is a perfectly good reason for someone to step closer.

The through line is simple: whether your language is plain or technical, people should be able to understand it — either on its own or in context.

It's a Filter, Not a Hook

A lot of marketing and branding experts will tell you to craft something memorable, something that grabs attention. That advice is usually right. Even on the sidewalk, you should not be boring.

But on the sidewalk, attention that converts to isn't the

goal; it's clarity. A hook tries to pull someone in. A filter lets people sort things out for themselves.

Sometimes clarity is interesting in its own right. And, if your work is compelling, your Sidewalk Statement won't be boring. A clear description of what you do will naturally spark curiosity. So, we are not trying to create a hook; we are simply being honest about the work we do. On the sidewalk, you don't need to manufacture intrigue when the work itself is intriguing.

It's worth repeating: a great Sidewalk Statement gives someone enough information to decide: *Is this something I care about?* If the answer is yes, they'll keep engaging. If the answer is no, they'll move on gracefully. Making space for both responses is an act of hospitality.

No Call to Action

The Sidewalk Statement is an identity statement. You're not really asking for anything. Instead, you're just answering a question.

This is where nonprofit leaders especially struggle. We're used to ending every communication with an ask. *Give now. Sign up. Learn more. Join us.* It's baked into how we've been trained to communicate.

But on the sidewalk, an ask is premature because you haven't earned it yet. If someone asks what you do and your answer ends with, "and you can learn more at our website," you've turned a conversation into a transaction. You've skipped past the human moment and jumped straight to marketing. People know when they are being marketed to; sometimes that's okay because they expect it. But the sidewalk is a place of conversation, not conversion.

Just tell them what you do. If they want to know more, they'll ask. Trust the statement to do its job. This is why we purposely decided not to call this a Sidewalk Pitch. That's what the elevator is for. Ok, it's not, the elevator is for standing there quietly and not making eye contact, but you get the point.

You can tell when someone is reciting from a script vs. speaking from the heart. Think of the last time you called a customer support line and the person on the other end was clearly reading from cue cards. When someone says, "Thank you for sharing that information with me" after every single thing you say, you absolutely know they are reading from a script. Honestly, it makes me crazy! Please talk to me like a human being!

This principle matters when you are creating a Sidewalk Statement. Speak like a human being, not like you're delivering a prescribed answer from a call center. It's fine to start writing your Sidewalk Statement on paper. But it's important that you make sure it works when spoken out loud. If it reads well on paper but feels awkward to say in conversation, it won't work.

Your Sidewalk Statement will live in conversations far more often than on a page. If it feels natural coming out of your mouth at a baseball game, in a checkout line, or at a dinner party, you've nailed it. If it sounds like you just recited the Pledge of Allegiance, you need to keep workshopping it.

Read it out loud and ask: Does it sound like something I would actually say? Or does it sound like something I'd read off the back of a brochure? If it feels rehearsed or stiff, keep working. The best Sidewalk Statements sound like they were never written down in the first place.

Two Models to Try

While there is no perfect formula for creating a Sidewalk Statement, there are a couple of practical fill-in-the-blank models you can use to get started. These models will help you craft a statement that is "speakable" and natural to share with others.

The Identity Approach:

In the identity approach, you focus on who you are and what you do that sets you apart. For example, our company, Liminal, is a branding agency. But we are more than that; we are a branding agency for nonprofits. That's a distinct position in the branding world and sets us apart from other agencies.

Now, there is more that makes us unique. We take a messaging-first approach and bring 50 combined years of experience leading and fundraising for nonprofit organizations. That's important. But on the sidewalk, none of that is urgent to share. That's for the elevator… or in our model, the Front Porch.

We are a nonprofit organization that [what you do].

- "We are a branding agency for nonprofits."
- "We are a nonprofit that connects families in New York City with safe, affordable housing."

The Action Approach:

We [action verb] so that [individuals/communities] experience [specific impact].

You can also take an action-based approach by focusing on what you actually do. This model shapes the statement around your work — what's unique about it and the impact it creates.

For example:

- "We walk with people in Des Moines toward sobriety."
- "We revive rivers to sustain wildlife and people."

Both approaches work. Use whichever feels more natural for your organization. The Identity Approach works well when what you are does most of the explaining. The Action Approach is ideal when what you do is the most compelling part of the story. You might even draft both versions, so you have each on hand, depending on the situation and your audience.

Test It

Finally, once you have a draft, test it. And test it often. Test it at the grocery store, the soccer field, a sales meeting, the next conference, or a local gathering. Just don't test it in the elevator!

Here's a simple way to know if it's working:

Say it out loud next time you are with someone who doesn't know your organization. This should not be a board member or colleague, but a friend, a neighbor, or someone at a coffee shop. To really gauge how it lands, choose someone who has no context for your work.

If they understand it immediately, you're close. If they nod and say, "Oh, cool," or ask a follow-up question, you're there. But if it goes over their head, if they furrow their brow, look confused, or say, 'So what does that mean, exactly?' — you definitely have some work to do.

The goal isn't a statement so comprehensive that no one ever asks a follow-up question. Some people will want to know more, and that's the whole point. The goal is a statement clear enough that a stranger knows whether they want to ask the next question.

Make It a Team Exercise

Crafting a Sidewalk Statement is an excellent exercise for your team to work on together. Gather five staff or board members in a room, explain what a Sidewalk Statement is, and share both models. Then, give them 10-20 minutes to write their own version independently. Then compare the results. Write them on a whiteboard or share them in the Zoom meeting.

You'll learn a lot about what people think your organization does. It's likely you'll find that everyone describes it differently. Some will default to insider language they didn't even *realize* was insider language. Don't be afraid to call that out! You may discover that the clearest, most compelling version comes from the newest person on the team, because they still remember what it was like not to know.

The best Sidewalk Statements often emerge when a team debates them together. So let that tension exist; it's productive because it pushes you to name what really matters.

Once you land on a statement the team can agree on, write it down and use it everywhere. Make sure everyone in your organization can say it without thinking, so the next time someone asks, "So what do you do?" the answer comes naturally, as if it had always been yours.

CHAPTER 8

A FINAL WALK THROUGH THE HOUSE

Practical Next Steps for Every Space

Years ago, I led a community-based organization where we built everything around the same framework you've been reading about in this book. We intentionally shaped a community that gave people space to belong at their own pace. We didn't push people into belonging, pressure them into deeper commitment, or force them through some kind of awkward "people funnel".

When someone was hanging out on the sidewalk or the front porch, we didn't treat them like they were somehow behind schedule or less important. We thoughtfully and intentionally built spaces that were clear, welcoming, and honest, and we trusted people to find their way into the community at their own pace.

Over the years, as we lived with this model, I began to notice something different in the way people talked about our community. They couldn't quite explain why it was different, but they knew it was. Many would tell me that it was the first time they had felt safe in a community like ours and that they had never really experienced anything quite like it before.

It wasn't because we had the biggest budget, the most Twitter followers, or a dope Instagram page. (Though if Instagram were around back then, I bet we could have pulled it off.) Our local art shows, concerts, fundraisers, and even our community engagement work were pretty epic.

While these things were cool and meaningful, the real difference maker in our community was that people hadn't been treated like unique human beings before in a context like ours. They had never been trusted to exist in a space in a way that made sense for their lives — without feeling like they were doing something wrong.

It's been years since this time, but people still tell me that experience changed how they think about belonging. One friend put it this way: "You ruined me for every other community, because nothing else feels the same." I've heard some version of that from more people than I can count. It wasn't magic; it was the framework that was consistently lived out.

Of course, not everyone loved that nonprofit community because it wasn't for everyone. There were people, often leaders and long-time members, who wanted us to push harder, move people faster, and prioritize the organization's growth at all costs. In effect, they wanted us to create a pipeline and measure success by how quickly people moved from the outside to the inside.

This is why the funnel that we talked about early in this book doesn't cultivate a welcoming nonprofit. It doesn't take into account that people can be trusted to move at their own pace. And trust is one of the keys to this framework's effectiveness. We have to trust that, most of the time, people know what's best for them.

When you force people to move at your pace, you don't create a sense of belonging. You might accomplish something out of sheer force of will. And yes, you can create momentum that way, but it won't be an authentic organization where people find true belonging and choose to invest in it. What those older metaphors produce is *compliance and obligation*. The difference is this: the people who stayed connected to our organization did so because they chose to, not because we engineered it.

One of the most important things I learned from Joseph Myers' *The Search to Belong* so many years ago was that he challenged a phrase I still hear all the time. He pointed out that leaders will often define for others what "true belonging" is supposed to look like.

It usually sounds something like this: *"If you really want to belong here, you need to [fill in the blank]."*

This fill-in-the-blank changes depending on the field, company, or organization. I grew up in the church, and in that context, it sounded like this: "If you want to belong here, you need to be part of a small group." I heard that exact sentence in multiple churches. It was so prevalent that the words never changed from one church to another.

I know I am not the only one who feels this way, but I loathe small groups. Like, I really, really hate them. I am sure they are fine for some people, but I have no interest in meeting up with a random group of people every Wednesday night – especially not in a setting where I was expected to take part in some kind of awkward forced intimacy with a bunch of people I barely knew.

I think I'd rather have a deep conversation with someone in an elevator.

What I learned, without anyone saying it directly, was that my refusal to fall in line made it clear that I did not really belong. And you know what? I did exactly what they were unintentionally inviting me to do.

I chose not to belong.

I am certain you've heard this same line of thinking at some point in your life. Maybe it happened on a nonprofit board: "If you really want to be part of the board, you need to be on the fundraising committee." Or maybe it's happened at an institution you thought you had a meaningful connection to: "If you really want to be a respected alumnus of this school, you'll donate to the new gymnasium".

Sometimes the message isn't that explicit, but most of the time it is. In fact, the message is consistently clear: if you won't do this one specific thing that we have decided is the most important way to contribute, you don't really belong here. That is defeating, and it's the exact opposite of genuine hospitality.

What Myers helped me see is that when someone doesn't belong in the way we've prescribed, it isn't a sign of their personal failure, selfishness, or lack of belief in the mission of the organization. It's a system design failure. And, if I'm being honest, it's a leadership failure.

The organization that decides that one space is the only space that counts is the one that sends the subtle message that we only want people who will belong in the way we prescribe.

I see this same dynamic play out in the nonprofit world today.

I first noticed it years ago at a major fundraising event in Philadelphia. I had the honor of attending a fundraiser for a well-known organization. They pulled out all the stops. They invited a prominent speaker and secured a classy, high-end venue near the Liberty Bell. The event was well organized, with over 400 people in attendance. Since I knew the Executive Director of the organization, I was aware that at least 15 to 20 high-net-worth individuals were in attendance, and that the organization had been building relationships with them all year. This was the big event that the entire development team had been working towards.

After the speaker told some powerful stories and energized the crowd, he made the ask. And this is where things went completely sideways for the development team. Instead of inviting transformational gifts from the donors who had been thoughtfully engaged all year, he asked for one thing: "What we're asking for tonight is a $50 monthly recurring donation from 200 people." And that was it.

To be clear, $10,000 in new recurring monthly revenue is meaningful. For many organizations, that's a win worth celebrating. Over the course of a year, that's $120,000 in new support. But at a large gala with major donors in the room—people capable of five- and six-figure gifts—that kind of total isn't transformative. It's modest.

The problem wasn't the monthly program. The problem was the mismatch. A single, narrow invitation defined belonging on one set of terms and left no room for those prepared to make a far larger investment. The ask fit one segment of the room, but it didn't account for the capacity of the major donors.

And when an invitation doesn't match the space someone is in, even generous people can walk away unsure if they belong.

You know what happened? Of the major donors in attendance, three signed up to be recurring donors, and the rest gave nothing that night. It's not that they didn't care about the mission; it's that the invitation didn't align with the space or with the kind of belonging they were looking for.

Of course, my friend was devastated. Over the next several weeks, he and his development team spent a lot of time reaching out to the major donors to reassure them that the gifts they had the capacity to make would be needed and appreciated.

And to be fair, the evening wasn't a total loss. Many others in the room—those whose capacity aligned with a $50 monthly commitment—did step forward. That was meaningful on its own.

But the donors who had come prepared to make transformational investments walked away confused because the organization had defined belonging on its own terms and failed to create space for their investment.

Think about how often we communicate, sometimes without even realizing it, that recurring giving is the only way to truly support our mission. Sure, we say there are other ways too, just go to a Ways to Give page on the website, and you'll see a lot of other options.

But the messaging is usually clear: *"If you really want to change lives and truly make a difference, become a monthly donor."*

Now, I believe monthly giving programs are incredibly valuable. I have been part of multiple nonprofits that have built creative, enduring monthly giving programs that sustain the work. These programs can generate predictable revenue, deepen donor commitment, and, when done well, give people a meaningful way to stay connected to your work over time. They are a legitimate and powerful tool for your nonprofit organization.

But they are *not* the only ways to belong to or support a nonprofit mission.

What about the contractor who gets paid irregularly and can't commit to a predictable monthly amount? What about the business owner whose income fluctuates season to season? What about the major donor who gives one significant gift a year and would find a $25/month ask almost insulting? What about the person who cares deeply about your work but simply doesn't have the financial capacity right now and could instead become one of your key volunteers?

When we create messaging that says "this is the most important way to belong," we unwittingly exclude those who might be able to contribute in other significant ways.

When we elevate one form of engagement as the "real" way to belong, we unintentionally tell everyone who doesn't fit that way of belonging that their contribution isn't enough. And we make them feel as though they're standing outside the house looking in.

This is the funnel talking and the pipeline at work. This thinking is exactly the kind of thing this book is asking you to leave behind. To be clear, I am not asking you to stop your monthly giving program. In fact, I strongly encourage you to start one today if you haven't already! There are incredible ways for people to get involved in your mission.[5]

But they are not the only way to 'really make a difference.' Saying so might help you build a recurring giving

---

[5] If you're looking to build or strengthen a monthly giving program, I'd recommend Dana Snyder's work at Positive Equation (positiveequation.com). She's helped dozens of nonprofits launch sustainable recurring-giving programs, and she is incredible at what she does. Tell her Liminal sent you.

program. But it won't help you build a welcoming non-profit. And honestly? That claim isn't even true. There are plenty of ways to have a real impact on real lives, other than being a recurring donor.

The truth is, when you start thinking in terms of relational spaces instead of funnel stages, people will notice. Unless they've read a 1,100-page book called *A Pattern Language* by a world-famous architect, they won't be able to name what's different. They won't say, "I appreciate that your organization honors the relational space I'm currently occupying." Of course, they won't because that would be totally weird.

But they will *feel* it because they will feel *seen*. When people are welcomed without pressure, they experience belonging, even if they're hanging out on the sidewalk a little longer than your strategic plan says they should.

And that feeling shapes how people view your organization. It's the difference between an organization people have an affinity for and one they tell their friends about. It's the difference between donors who give as little as they can and those who give because they know they are valued as real partners. It's the difference between a community people simply pass through and one they never want to leave.

Before we close out this book, I want to walk back through the house one more time. Not to cover it all again. The old adage still holds true: People need to be reminded more often than they need to be instructed. But I do want to leave you with something practical for each space. Frameworks like this are only as useful as what you do with them on Monday morning.

So, let's take one more walk through the house before we decide whether to buy it.

The Sidewalk: Just Say It.

Yes, I am channeling my inner Nike here by riffing off of their "Just Do It" tagline — what's a sneaker head from the Portland-Metro area supposed to do?

If you worked through Chapter 7, you have a head start on crafting an effective Sidewalk Statement. One sentence that is 15 words or fewer that you can say at a baseball game, in a checkout line, or at a conference without sounding like you're reading off a brochure.

Now, start saying it. Just Do It.

And remember, we called it a Sidewalk Statement, not a Sidewalk Pitch. You're not selling anything. You're just telling people what you do and trusting them to decide what to do with it.

Make sure your website's homepage, especially the hero section, reflects that same clarity. If someone lands on your site and can't tell what you do within three to five seconds, your digital sidewalk needs some serious attention. Go ahead, pull up your homepage right now and ask yourself: Does this read like a Sidewalk Statement, or like a Kitchen Table conversation?

If it's the latter, you've already lost most of the people who are walking by.

The same goes for your social media bios, email signatures, and how your team talks about the organization at events. Consistency matters because if five people on your staff describe your work five different ways, you have a sidewalk problem, and more urgently, it means you have a clarity problem.

A note about AI and the sidewalk: This is the one space where AI can genuinely help. Use it to test variations of your statement. Ask it to simplify your language. Let it pressure-test whether your homepage copy is clear to someone with no context. AI is great at helping you find the simplest way to describe what you do. Just make sure the final version sounds like a human, not a chatbot.

The Front Porch: Welcome Like You Mean It

Here's an exercise that might make you uncomfortable: sign up for your own email list. Make a small donation to your own organization. Then sit back and pay attention to what happens next.

Better yet, ask a friend, someone no one in your organization knows, to do the same. Give it a week or two, then interview them about their experience.

Here are some questions to ask:

- What was your impression of the first email you received?

- Did it feel like a warm welcome, or did it read like a financial receipt?

- Is there a human voice in it, or does it sound like it was generated by a robot in your CRM software?

- Did the response to your donation make you feel valued?

- Or, did you feel like you were being pushed further down a funnel?

The front porch is where most nonprofits lose people. We spend so much energy on the sidewalk (getting attention) and the living room (deepening relationships) that we forget about the people standing right in front of us, the ones who just took their first step a little bit closer. That step is riskier than you think because it opens people up to receiving more from you. More emails, more invitations, and hopefully not more spam.

If you are going to rewrite one thing this week, start with your welcome email or your first-time donor thank-you. Make it sound like it came from someone who noticed someone had shown up and was genuinely glad they did. Make sure that this communication shows them how valued they are, and make sure it's clear that they know just how incredibly valuable they are.

If AI has enough context about who you are, it can help you draft the first version, and it's actually a decent tool for this purpose. But review the draft, read it out loud. If it sounds like something you'd never actually say to a person on your porch, rewrite it in your own voice. The draft is a starting point, an outline, a super rough draft, even. It is definitely not a finished product.

The bottom line is this: Welcome without pressure. Don't follow up a first-time $25 donation immediately with a request to join your monthly giving program. That's the equivalent of someone stepping onto your porch and you immediately asking them to move in. Give them space to look around, get comfortable, feel valued and known. You'll know when the time is right to invite them further into the house.

The Living Room: Tell the Real Story

If the front porch is where you welcome people, the living room is where you let them see who you really are.

Pull up the last three emails you sent to your donors or volunteers. Read them again with fresh eyes. Do they sound like press releases, or do they sound like a friend catching up with you over coffee? Is there a real story in there, or is it just metrics and outcomes wrapped in nice formatting?

Living room communication should feel like you are pulling back the curtain. Not in a way that's reckless or oversharing, but in a way that shows people you trust them with the fuller picture of your work. That might mean sharing a story about a challenge, alongside the success. It could mean introducing the people behind the work, not just the programs and the metrics. It could also mean telling donors what their support actually made possible, in a way that's specific and sincere, not polished and generic.

The living room is where I would use AI with caution: it's tempting to use it to polish your updates so that they sound smooth and professional. To the best of your ability, resist that urge. In the living room, a little imperfection can be a signal of trust. A handwritten note with a little sloppy (yet legible) handwriting is more powerful than a perfectly formatted email or form letter. A handwritten P.S. after the signature line that feels spontaneous can mean more than a professionally designed infographic. Your donors don't need perfection; they need to see you as a real person.

And remember who the hero is! In your living room stories, the people your organization serves are the heroes. Your donors and your organization are the guides. When you get this right, your storytelling changes. It stops being about what your organization accomplished and starts being about what became possible because real people showed up for one another and made a difference in the world.

Effort Signals: Establishing Trust in an AI-Assisted World

Your donors can sense when something feels off. A message that's too polished, too generic, or too frequent can trigger suspicion: "Did a human actually write this? Do they actually care?"

AI makes communication easier, but ease can backfire if it erodes the sense that real people are behind the work.

Here are a few ways to signal genuine effort, even when AI is part of your process:

1. **Name the author.** When sharing updates, reports, or appeals, make it clear who the author is. "Our team reviewed this quarter's impact data and wanted to share what stood out." The point is: don't let your communications feel like they came from a faceless organization. Put a name or a team on it.

2. **Show your work.** When appropriate, be transparent: "We used AI to help us identify themes in your feedback, then our staff shaped what you're reading." Honesty builds trust.

3. **Add imperfection.** Not every message needs to be flawless. A handwritten note, a typo you didn't catch, a P.S. that feels spontaneous. These things signal that a person was here. Don't over-polish everything.

4. **Match effort to space.** A mass email on the Sidewalk can lean on AI. A thank-you to a Living Room donor should feel personal. A Kitchen Table conversation should never feel automated.

The goal isn't to hide AI. It's to make sure the humans in your organization stay visible.

The Kitchen Table: Show Up Honestly

This is the space where most nonprofit leaders hold back. It's vulnerable to sit across from a major donor or a board member and say, "I'll be honest, what we're trying is not working. Here's what's keeping me up at night, and these are the areas where we need help."

But the people at your Kitchen Table didn't pull up a

chair for a polished presentation. They sat down for the truth. And if you can't trust the people at your Kitchen Table with the truth, you have the wrong people at the Kitchen Table.

At your next board meeting or major donor conversation, try sharing one real challenge you're facing alongside your wins. It doesn't have to be the biggest challenge, at least not yet. It definitely should not be a manufactured vulnerability designed to lead into an ask. It needs to be an actual, honest challenge. Ask for input, not just money. The people at the Kitchen Table are not only interested in funding your mission, they are there to help you think through your challenges, strategize, and develop solutions.

This is the one space where AI has no business running the show. AI can help you prep talking points or organize your financial data (but be careful with this!) before a meeting. But the conversation and tone of the meeting need to come from you. Kitchen Table trust is built on the belief that a human is on the other side of the table, being honest about what's hard and hopeful about what's possible. No algorithm can manufacture that.

A final reminder: not everyone belongs at your Kitchen Table, and that's okay. This space is for the people who have earned it through sustained trust and mutual investment. Inviting someone to the Kitchen Table before they're ready doesn't honor them; it overwhelms them. Let people arrive at the table in their own time.

Pulling It All Together

If you want a practical way to use this framework starting this week, here's what I'd suggest:

Take a campaign or initiative and map every message to the Sidewalk, Front Porch, Living Room, and Kitchen Table. It might be your year-end appeal or spring gala. It could be your next newsletter or quarterly update. For each piece of communication, ask: Who is this for? What space are they in? Does the tone fit the context, and does the invitation match that space?

If your year-end email reads the same whether it's going to a first-time website visitor or a long-term recurring donor, something's off. The message itself might be fine, but it's landing in four different spaces, and each space needs a different version of that story.

You don't have to overhaul everything at once. You can start with one space and get that right, and then move to the next.

A Final Tool: The Spaces Cheat Sheet

Before you close this book, I want to leave you with something you can pin to the bulletin board, hand to your team, or refer to before you hit "send" on your next email.

Summarize each space on one page: Who's here, what they need, how we connect, the messaging focus, and the invitation. Post it where your communications, fundraising, and program teams can see it. Use it as a gut-check before every campaign, every update, every conversation.

Scan the QR code below to download a printable one-page cheat sheet for your team. It summarizes each space: who's here, what they need, how we connect, the messaging focus, and the invitation.

The goal isn't to follow this framework perfectly. The goal is to see people differently and stop asking, "How do we move donors through our funnel?" and start asking, "What space are they in, and how do we show up well and meet them in that space?"

When you do that, something shifts. Your communications will feel less like marketing and more like hospitality. Your donors will seem less like ATMs and more like people. And your organization will begin to resemble a home instead of a factory.

That's the work.

Now, go create spaces that people want to belong to.

CONCLUSION

"Gordon wants to build a computer for all the other people who build computers. I want to build something for people who never thought they'd want a computer... something that makes people fall in love."

— Cameron Howe, *Halt and Catch Fire*[6]

Clearly, this book hasn't been about building computers, but too often in nonprofit communications and donor relations, we build like Gordon.

---

[6] It's worth noting that *Halt and Catch Fire* is my favorite show of all time. Set in the early days of personal computing, it follows a group of visionaries trying to build something meaningful. It's about the beauty and struggle of creating in a world that doesn't always get it which, to me, makes it the perfect metaphor for nonprofit work. I'm currently on my fifth rewatch and I still discover something new every time.

We design our websites, messaging, and donor strategies for ourselves, or worse, for our peers. We build to impress other professionals, win over internal boards, or gain approval within the nonprofit sector.

In doing so, we create marketing materials that make sense to *us*, but we miss the chance to connect with donors and potential supporters. Often, we do this without even realizing it.

Regardless of our level of awareness, we need a different approach.

We need ways of communicating that invite real people into something more human and authentic — something that adds meaning to their lives and connects with their stories and pace of life.

This approach will help us create nonprofit organizations that people want to connect with.

It will help us craft communications that feel natural, generous, and honest so supporters can engage in a way that fits *them*.

These ideas are also about something even more significant: *Who gets to define what belonging looks like?*

Too often, institutions try to define belonging on their own terms: Give here. Show up there. Stay engaged in the ways we've decided matter most.

But real belonging doesn't work like that.

We don't get to decide if someone belongs.

They do.

Just because someone donates doesn't mean they feel connected. And just because someone hasn't given a dollar doesn't mean your mission isn't already influencing their life.

Our job isn't to control the relationship.

It's to create space.

To make room for connection.

To cultivate organizational belonging with clarity and care so that, when people choose to lean in, they *know* they're welcome.

So, let's get to work building nonprofit organizations people want to belong to.

Just keep quiet on those elevators.

ABOUT THE AUTHOR

Todd Hiestand has spent over two decades building communities and helping nonprofits do the same.

He co-founded and led a community-based nonprofit organization for 14 years, learning firsthand what it takes to welcome strangers, nurture belonging, and establish a sustainable base of support from the ground up.

He has served as a development director, led multi-channel fundraising campaigns, and worked alongside hundreds of nonprofit teams across the country to help them communicate their mission with greater clarity and conviction.

Today, Todd is co-founder and co-principal of Liminal, a brand strategy and communications agency serving nonprofits navigating critical moments of transition. His work focuses on helping mission-driven organizations move through "liminal spaces", the complex, often uncomfortable seasons between where they are and where they need to be.

Todd holds a Master's degree and speaks regularly on nonprofit brand clarity, fundraising, and organizational growth.

He and his wife, Melanie, live in the suburbs of Portland, Oregon, with four sons, 12 Goat Yoga goats, nine ducks, 18 chickens, five dogs, a lizard, a turtle, and a rabbit.

www.ingramcontent.com/pod-product-compliance
Lightning Source LLC
Chambersburg PA
CBHW070758260726
48660CB00005B/1679